What Begins Here
Transforms the World

by
Debbie Salter Goodwin

2019-20 NMI
MISSION EDUCATION RESOURCES

Books

TRACY SAHIB, SERVANT OF CHRIST IN INDIA
by Olive G. Tracy
Edited by R. Franklin Cook

SHIRO KANO
Faithfulness at Any Price
by Alice Spangenberg
Edited by Merritt Nielson

WHAT BEGINS HERE TRANSFORMS THE WORLD
by Debbie Salter Goodwin

What Begins Here Transforms the World

by
Debbie Salter Goodwin

NAZARENE MISSIONS INTERNATIONAL

Dedication

This book is dedicated to the committed faculty and staff at Africa Nazarene University who have taken on the school's transformational motto as a personal calling. You are the heroes of this story. And to the students who demonstrate the difference that a life transformed by God can make, may you see the fruit of your persistent labor and be fulfilled but never satisfied. May all who enter Africa Nazarene University catch the same vision and become the God-transformed agents this world desperately needs.

Table of Contents

About the Author

Debbie Salter Goodwin has been writing for the Church of the Nazarene for more than forty years. Her stories of missionaries and international laypersons have appeared in Holiness Today. Two of her Christian parenting books have been translated into several languages. Her weekly blog, Quiet Circle, shares a spiritual respite for anyone who needs a green pasture. She lives north of Atlanta, Georgia, USA, with her husband, Mark, who retired from 40 years of pastoral ministry in four churches. Together they continue to find ways to be transforming agents wherever God leads them.

Acknowledgements

When I volunteered to join Portland, Oregon's First Church of the Nazarene's IT Work & Witness team traveling to Africa Nazarene University (ANU) to install security cameras in October 2017; I went as a writer. I planned to interview faculty, staff, and students and tell stories that hadn't been shared with the global church. I met with Rob North, Director of University Advancement, when he presented at Portland First. He caught my vision and helped me make critical connections from the beginning. One of those was with Amy Crofford, whom I knew only as a byline on children's missionary books. She was invaluable as she helped me make interview appointments before I arrived. This book could not have been as complete without her help.

I had met Vice-Chancellor Leah Marangu when she and her husband were at Olivet Nazarene College (now University in Bourbonnais, Illinois, USA) at the same time I taught there. It was a sweet reunion and a joy to celebrate her 21-year legacy as she retired. To be able to meet and interview the new vice-chancellor, Dr. Bhebhe, was another high point. I hope I did justice to the experience and passion he brings to this new responsibility.

I am grateful to every faculty and staff member who granted me time for an interview. I appreciate each student who impressed me with how they embraced the transformational vision when I didn't even ask about it.

To Rod Reed, deputy vice-chancellor, who took time to review my outlines and shared his wisdom and perspective in helpful ways, thank you! And to get-it-done Carla Frazier, who took my list of questions and tracked down every detail or statistic, I would work with you on any project!

I visited ANU as a curious spectator and do not pretend to know the school, as well as those who teach, study, or work there. For that reason, I tried to research, define, collaborate, and question everything I wrote. Still, there may be some discrepancies. Just hear my heart. There is a story of transformation at Africa Nazarene University. It is a story that Nazarene Missions began, and your prayers and contributions make possible. You need to hear that story. That's why I share it.

Debbie Goodwin
Roswell, Georgia, 2018

Editor's Note:

Many who will read this book will find connections to the stories presented here. Africa Nazarene University is today the result of many investments from across the global Nazarene family. Some have contributed funds to see ANU built. Others have gone on Work & Witness trips to ANU and have invested blood, sweat, and tears to see the buildings that grace the campus of ANU rise from the Kenyan landscape. Whatever your part in it, Africa Nazarene University, with its mission to transform the world, is possible because of the faithfulness of many who sacrificed to see ANU come to maturity for the sake of Africa and the world into which it sends its graduates. The vignettes presented in this book represent some who came to ANU with faith and others who came to faith through ANU. Read with delight at the transformations God has wrought.

Chapter 1

Where Transformation Begins

Kendi [KEN-dee] Muchungi [moo-CHOONG-gee], class of 2001, is a blur of color as she rushes back to her office in the Computer Science Department at Africa Nazarene University (ANU) in Kenya where she has taught since January 2016. It is a sun-bleaching day. Students find the breeze blowing through Helstrom Chapel or sit under the red-flowered Nandi [NAHN-dee] Flame trees planted for days like these.

For a few stolen minutes, Kendi just sits. She stares at the diploma hanging on the wall announcing her Ph.D. degree from the University of Surrey in England. Those days haunt her but in a good way. She still thinks about the research she did to produce a computerized retinal prototype as a fore-runner for an artificial retinal implant. But her research had only gone so far. She considered the blind and nearly blind who struggle in a world created with so much to see and wondered when she could return to the research that could transform their world.

Kendi is just one example of the sixty full-time lecturers and around one hundred twenty part-time lecturers who bring their Christian commitment and intellectual curiosity mixed with a healthy desire to use what they know to inspire students to change some part of their world. It isn't by accident that when many of them landed as students at ANU, a desire to give back to the University began to grow so deeply that many stayed to teach or work at the University. In fact, about twenty percent of the faculty and staff are graduates of ANU. They stay not because they can't go somewhere else. They stay because of the Christian ethos and environment they found that helped them establish their faith and grow. They see transformation in front of their eyes, and they want to be a part of it.

Transformation is the heart and soul of Africa Nazarene University.

What Begins Here Transforms the World

Transformation is the heart and soul of Africa Nazarene University. "What begins here transforms the world" is the motto that appears on their documents.

However, it has become more than that. It has become their mission. And it couldn't happen at a more unlikely place. Located in the middle of the great Maasai [mah-SIE] savannah, the campus settled on one hundred twenty-four acres of the expansive grassland, not quite desert but not natural garden either. Drive twenty-four kilometers (about 15 miles) south of the bustling capital city of Nairobi [nie ROH-bee] where most of the four million people who live there are under the age of 30.[1] ANU offers more than a liberal arts education to the 3,600 students enrolled; the school offers community, an invested faculty, and the possibility of life transformation.

While intellectual pursuit and career development are important, it is not what built this school. With the first shovelful of dirt in the early 1990s to build a campus for the Church of the Nazarene in northern Africa, ANU understood that transformation begins in the heart. It is their fervent goal that every student be exposed to the Gospel. Jesus' call and commission gives life and purpose to this motto.

How do they turn a motto into a life calling?

"A lot of it is just repetition, repetition, repetition. But it helps when you believe in it," says Deputy Vice-Chancellor Rod Reed. He's right. Spend any time on campus, read any of their literature and the words leap off the page as you see students taking the motto as their life mission.

For sure, Kenya is a country that could use transformation. Take her land. Only 9.5% of the country's land is farmable.[2] Those who do farm raise crops and animals to

---

[1] "2018 World Population by Country (Live)." *World Population Review*. www.worldpopulationreview.com.

[2] Major Problems Facing Kenya Today." *AfricaW: Africa and the World*. Unless otherwise stated, the statistics in this chapter are taken from this article. www.africaw.com/major-problems-facing-kenya-today

feed themselves. Unpredictable climate reversals can wipe out a family's meal ticket leaving them with no backup plan.

Or consider the forty different ethnic groups in Kenya alone. Tribalism cannot be ignored. It fuels political rivalry, boundary disputes, and generational revenge.

It might surprise you that 82.5 percent of the Kenyan population identify themselves as Christian with more Protestants than Catholics. Because of that Kenya is often quoted as being one of the most Christian of all the countries in Africa. However, it also carries the dubious label as being one of the most politically corrupt countries. Transparency International is a global organization that "works with governments, businesses, and citizens to stop the abuse of power bribery and secret deals." They rank Kenya's corruption perception as 143 out of 180 countries on their 2017 Corruption Perception Index.[3]

Perhaps one of the most hopeful facts about Kenya is its high literacy rate. While many African students graduate from a Kenya-based university, they are not always able to put their degree to work because of the disconnect between their course work and the job market.[4] They can easily become part of the fifty percent of Kenyans who live below the poverty line, and end up jobless on the streets with a college diploma in their pocket.

---

[3] "Corruption Perceptions Index 2017," *Transparency International*. www.transparency.org/news/feature/corruption_perceptions _index _2017

[4] Okoti, Daisy, (1 June, 2018) "It Takes More than a Degree to Beat Unemployment." *Daily Nation*. www.nation.co.ke/lifestyle/mynet-work/It-takes-more-than-a-degree-to-beat-unemployment/ 3141096-4588296-ff7uv4/index.html

Another harsh reality in this developing country is their high HIV/AIDS rate among adults. Almost 1.6 million adults are affected out of their 51 million inhabitants.

And what is true in Kenya is reproduced throughout other countries where students come to attend ANU.

No one considers it an accident that Africa Nazarene University was planted in this melting pot of poverty, underused resources, high literacy, Christian affinity, and political corruption. But how could transformation become more than just a sound bite or a good piece of propaganda? They had to give it feet as well as wings. They began to look for ways the campus could become a laboratory for transformation, a place where students could participate in activities that led to transformation of the heart as well as the head.

When you hear about the technology, the think tanks, the national and international competitions students are exposed to in this developing country, it's not hard to see them as Davids facing the Goliaths of their home countries. When you realize how many students find their anchor in Christ during Holiness Week or connect to the heart of Christ and the needs of people during Impact Week, you begin to realize just how seriously they take this transformational mission. Students are not just trying to graduate with a money-making degree; they actually believe they can change some part of their world.

Can they? They may not be able to change the statistics that continue to pull their country or continent down, but they can transform places. They are becoming transformational catalysts for people. They are making a difference, and that difference will change someone's world.

ANU focuses on transformation in three ways. They encourage all students to:

- Embrace the life-changing power of salvation through Jesus and empowerment through the Holy Spirit.
- Develop a character of godly integrity, competence in skills, and living it out in community with those who share it and need it.
- Internalize transformation as a life mission to "Be the change you want to see!" for someone or some group.

What begins here, transforms the world!

Take a walk down any of the streets or paths on campus, and you will probably see one of the poster-covered towers bearing the motto. Step into one of the fifty buildings, and you will find it on walls. Attend chapel, and you will hear it repeated at least once if not multiple times. Talk to students about what they want to do after graduation, and they will echo this same goal. The statement is everywhere. *What begins here transforms the world.* And when you hear it, it doesn't come out forced or artificial. They mean it whether it comes from administrators, faculty, staff, or students.

"When you have a key, you have a way in," Chaplain Cindy North said as she delivered a message during one chapel. She was talking more than just about keys to locked doors of cultural acceptance or political accomplishment. She wanted them to know that the first open door is through Jesus. When Mary (Miss ANU, 2017-18) said with determination dripping from every word, "I'm meant to serve God," it makes you look at how deep your own commitment goes.

How do you cultivate this transformational climate? How do you pass on more than a motto? How do you get students to graduate with a "give-back" mentality? How can anyone face the odds that Kenya and many other challenged countries face and be hopeful?

It is almost an oxymoron that in the middle of a country challenged in every way, ANU rises as an oasis of hope. But hope doesn't just exist there; hope soars.

So how did it all begin? What vision made it possible to take a simple motto and make it a mission? For that story, we will turn back the clock and step onto the land before there was a blueprint or a classroom.

Chapter 2

From Mudhole to Mission

Stand in the middle of open country where the Rift Valley runs north to south in Kenya with its steep cliffs and where the Athi [AH-zee] River flows. You would see what this land looked like before the Church of the Nazarene planted a university there. You would see zebras cavort on their way to the river at the base of rock cliffs where the monkeys live and play. You would watch the March to May rains wash away anything that might try to take hold and grow. In the summer, when the bold and burning sun dehydrated anything not adapted to desert living, you would wonder what would survive.

Into this empty land, mission-minded leaders of the Church of the Nazarene, both missionary and Kenyan, envisioned how they could transform the land, build a campus, develop a curriculum of study, and open their doors to anyone wanting a chance to become a transformational agent. When Kenya passed the University Act of 1985 giving permission to establish private universities, Nazarene leadership knew they had their northern target for an educational center for the Church of the Nazarene. The 1993 Nazarene General Assembly unanimously approved the new school plant, and the Kenyan Government granted the same. Named Africa Nazarene University in order to meet continental needs beyond the reach of Kenya, ANU became the first private university not connected to an existing university to receive this credentialing from Kenya and the first liberal arts university for the Church of the Nazarene outside of North America. Dr. Martha John became the first vice-chancellor and opened the school to sixty-two students from eleven countries in 1994. Two years later, Professor[5] Leah Marangu [mah-RAHNG-goo] was installed as vice-chancellor to begin twenty-one years of legacy, growth, innovation, and history-making firsts for the Church of the Nazarene as well as Kenya.

Today, you can take that drive to Africa Nazarene University from Nairobi on its bumpy, sometimes cattle-invaded road with roughly built business shacks advertising everything from barber services to fast food. However, as soon as you drive through the gate that reads Africa Nazarene University, the scene changes. Painted block cement buildings with their brick-colored roofs stand three and four stories

---

[5] Professor is the highest title given to someone who fulfilled specific academic requirements. It acknowledges that a person has more than a Ph.D.

with offices and classrooms. Green grass is a carpet of contrast to the buildings. Stone pathways lead students, faculty, and staff to walk past roses and other flowering plants and shrubs. It is a garden so unexpected in this undeveloped place that you can't help but step back and wonder…how did this oasis come to be?

To tell part of the story, you need to know how Professor Leah Marangu, a Kenyan woman, broke barriers and opened doors for women and others as she set out to make a difference in the land of her birth. Her goal was peace in a conflict torn environment. Her dream was beauty in a desolate land. Her mission was transformation by God's design and leadership.

To begin that journey Professor Marangu and her husband, John, wanted to pursue education that would help them contribute and improve learning in Kenya. They decided to pack up family and belongings and find education in the United States in 1960, settling in the Olivet Nazarene College community. Leah wanted to pursue nursing as a way to make a difference in her country. Since Olivet didn't have a nursing program at that time, she applied at a nearby Catholic school. However, they denied her application. The school was governed by different perceptions about women at that time and did not believe that Leah would have the years to invest her degree because of her responsibilities as wife and mother. Instead, Leah joined her husband at Olivet and enrolled in home economics so that she could take back to her country information that would transform lives with preventive health and nutrition.

After they both graduated from Olivet with bachelor's degrees, they pursued master's degrees at Northern Illinois University and Ph.D.'s from Iowa State University. Then, they returned to Olivet where John taught biology and Leah taught in the local school district.

Her years at Olivet taught her more than nutrition. She saw the multi-layered educational thrust of a liberal arts college. She recognized how Olivet taught pastors as fervently as it taught other disciplines. The model inspired her in ways that would change the trajectory of her life and the life of Nazarene education in Kenya. In fact, in the early days of the university, leadership wanted to cap enrollment at 200 for fear of growing past their ability to manage effectively. But Professor Marangu knew that God told her, "You didn't come back from America to serve only 200 students." God had bigger plans.

Professor Marangu officiates at her last graduation.

As Professor Marangu stepped into her office for the last weeks of her twenty-one years at Africa Nazarene University, she couldn't keep from making another walk to the window with a view on her campus world. She always loved seeing students hurrying to classes, a few in casual conversations, others in study groups. The sight that always took her breath away was the beauty of the student-pummeled stone path spoking from the clock tower. She looked at these paths and remembered how many university students in the '90s rioted and threw stones to protest everything from academic interference to politically charged issues. She always told ANU students that

> Stones are not for throwing on people. Stones are God's resources. We use God's resources for beauty and functionality. ANU students have a mission, and that mission is to serve God and serve humanity. So, we crush stones and make beauty.

And they did. They chiseled and crushed the stones removed from the land during the excavation for building. They created a labyrinth that still directs feet to halls of learning and altars of prayer.

Professor Marangu smiled at the flowering bushes and plants that bordered the pathways, a veritable garden in the middle of desert. How many of them did she put in her own trunk and carry here for planting? Nearly all of them, she remembered. Each bush and plant was like one of her children, something to nurture and help grow.

When she started as vice-chancellor in 1996, there were not quite one hundred students and only three study programs. Today, there are nearly 3,600 registered students on two campuses studying in 40 programs in several disciplines. That's a lot of growth in twenty-one years!

Not only did this Kenyan woman break records on campus, but Professor Leah Marangu also broke records in Kenya. She was the first Kenyan woman to rise to the ranks of a full professor at a university in Kenya. She was the first woman to be named vice-chancellor of a higher education institution and first Kenyan woman to receive a Ph.D. She has received twenty national and international awards. Each of the three Kenyan presidents in office during Professor Marangu's chancellorship awarded her the country's highest medals: the Silver Star of Kenya, the Moran of the Order of the Burning Spear, and the Order of the Burning Spear. According to the National Honours Act, these awards go to people who exhibit "exemplary qualities, or achievements of heroism, patriotism or leadership, one who has made an exemplary contribution to the country." [6] However, Professor Marangu never tried to win awards; she was simply trying to transform her world.

An original painting of a lion and her cubs hung in the Board Room during her leadership years. Olive Mugenda [moo-GEN-dah], vice-chancellor of Kenyatta [ken-YAH-tah] University, the third largest university in Kenya, presented it to her mentor, Professor Marangu. The painting was a metaphor of the mentoring a young

[6] Muchiri, Marikio. "What Presidential Awards, Orders, and Medals Mean." Posted 21 August 2018. *Kenyans.co.ke*. hwww.kenyans.co.ke/news/what-presidential-awards-orders-and-medals-kenya-mean-0

educator received from Professor Marangu. In addition to Vice-Chancellor Mugenda, there was Professor Kobia [KOH-bee-yah], a former student of Professor Marangu. Margaret Kobia has served as chairperson of the Public Service Commission until nominated to serve on the president's cabinet in January, 2018. These are only two of the women who came after Professor Marangu to head universities and governmental commissions, something that was not possible before Professor Marangu opened doors that had been closed to women.

Vice-chancellor Marangu became more than an institutional administrator keeping her academic thumb in everyone's back. Students lovingly called her ANU's mother. Many experienced her nurture and mentoring.

The walls of her office became a scrapbook of the years. There are pictures of the mudhole that became a road leading into the campus. There are pictures of the graduation gatherings at the clock tower before there was grass. There is the picture of her husband with the cane he used to drive away snakes behind the building site for Helstrom Student Centre. Perhaps the pictures of zebras and giraffes roaming freely on the land behind the university tell the biggest story of transformation. "Yes, it is a wonderful story of transformation," Professor Marangu echoes as she returns to her desk to begin hand-signing every one of the 1,072 certificates of graduation stacked on her desk. They will be her last.

I wanted to have an education that cares about people.

"My leadership style is people-oriented" she explains. Students, faculty, and staff would agree. Her door was always open as was her heart. She dispensed wisdom and courage and prayer as often as she signed her name to official documents and decisions. "I wanted to have an education that cares about people. I had it in my heart [to] develop a crop of leaders that are not self-seeking."

On October 31, 2017, Professor Marangu retired to enter a new season of life. She packed up pictures and mementos that brought back scenes she would always remember. In honor of her extraordinary service to the mission of ANU, the Board of Trustees named the residential campus after her. It is just another way that Leah T. Marangu will always be a part of the land and the people who work and learn there.

However, the life and impact of Africa Nazarene University is not wrapped up in one person. It takes everyone. The competent administration, faculty, and staff make ANU a distinguished place of higher learning in Kenya, but what happens at ANU goes beyond competency. Their transformational mission influences the way faculty teach and how students learn. Problem-solving becomes a priority. When faculty and students catch this vision and apply it to real-life problems, their stories inspire and convict. Impact Week is a good place to begin.

Chapter 3
Where Problem-solving Impacts

There is an encouraging new interest among college and university students to address the issues that challenge life on this planet. International organizations have taken note and have created opportunities for competition and engagement. They seek to help students combine their skills with problem-solving techniques and apply them to global issues.

Impact Week

Impact Week is the name of the organization that ANU has participated with since 2015. It began in Germany with some forward-thinking entrepreneurs and innovation consultants and has grown with an extensive global reach. The organization unites people from different countries to "foster innovation, entrepreneurship, and intercultural exchange through Design Thinking."[7] Trained coaches identify a target country, accept applications, and coach teams in the process of Design Thinking in order to discover new solutions. Mr. James Obuhuma [oh-boo-HOO-mah], IT lecturer, and Dr. Kendi Muchungi (see Chapter 1), both from the Computer and Information Technology Department, have served as senior Design Thinking coaches.

Design Thinking is a specific problem-solving philosophy that surfaced in the 1950s. It takes a problem-solving team through a defined process to find an innovative solution that fits the context and is potentially sustainable. Impact Week teaches Design Thinking and then coaches problem-solving sessions using this formulated approach. One factor that makes it a perfect match for solving social problems is its emphasis on empathizing with the people struggling or victimized by the problem. This protects problem solvers from a clinical or generic solution. It has to fit real people in real contexts.

After the ANU team participated in the training of a Kenya-based Impact Week, they brought Impact Week to their own campus in 2016. One hundred twenty people developed seventeen business models and pitched them to judges. Five teams won money that would give them a chance to try their idea. One winning team called themselves Team Happy Farm and pitched an idea for a "farm in a box" that a recipient could use to take a small piece of unused land and grow sufficient produce from it to help feed people who didn't have enough to exist.

---

[7] *Impact Week*. www.impactweek.net

In November of 2017, ANU hosted Impact Week using the organization's trainers while mentoring their own. Fifty-six students participated with eight coaches and came up with eight new ideas. In 2018, ANU launched their independent Impact Week and expects to make it an annual event.

The good news is that Impact Week has an impact that lasts more than a week. Students take what they learn and invest it in their community. For example, one group organized themselves as Squadron One to take Design Thinking into area high schools. They tailored the coaching from Impact Week to fit high school students in a fun and easy way.

But Impact Week is just one transformational tool.

The John Ngila Story

When John Ngila [eng-GEE-lah] visited ANU's campus for the first time in 2011, he knew he didn't need to visit another campus. He was looking for the right Christian educational environment to finish his degree in international business. He knew he had found what he was looking for as he walked the spoked paths of the interior campus. "If ANU could make an oasis out of a wilderness," he thought, "they could bring the best out of me as well." He's never questioned his decision to stay.

> If ANU could make an oasis out of a wilderness, they could bring the best out of me as well.

After finishing his degree in 2014, he stayed at ANU as an administrative assistant in the Business School. It was

John Ngila's chance to give back in a way that would move students farther, the way ANU had motivated him.

John remembered how his classes emphasized "sustainable development goals" in business. John prefers the term "social entrepreneurship." He explains that "The difference between entrepreneurship and social entrepreneurship is [whether] entrepreneurs care about profits only. Social entrepreneurs take care of the planet and the people [before] the profits." It was another way he found ANU to be fertile soil for the difference he wanted to be a part of.

The Hult Prize Competition

The Hult Prize Competition was a perfect match for John's social entrepreneurial passion. It was established in 2010 by Swede Bertil Hult [buhr-TIL HUHLT] to offer college students a chance to solve world problems by using a sustainable business model. It has morphed into a cooperative between the Hult International Business School, the United Nations Foundation, and the Clinton Global Initiative. The Hult family donates 1 million dollars a year to provide start-up money for winning teams to launch their business ideas. What better way to give students a chance to transform their world? John became campus director and key trainer for the competition.

The Hult Competition has been called "the Nobel Prize for Students" and has been featured in a TIME Magazine Cover Story highlighting the "Top 5 Ideas Changing the

World"[8] The competition engages the best and brightest from international schools. The Foundation selects a world problem for the teams to study and develop a sustainable business idea that will help solve the problem. ANU would have a steep learning curve.

During the four years that ANU has been involved in this competition, 190 four-member teams competed at the campus level to involve 760 students in this competition at some level. Four winning teams have gone on to regionals in Dubai [doo-BIE] and Nairobi. Those who placed in regionals earned admittance to an eight-week business incubator where teams received intense coaching to refine their ideas and business models before presenting in the regional finals.

Team Taka Smart

Clement was captain for ANU's Taka Smart [TAH-kah SMAHRT] team. *Taka* means waste in Swahili [swah-HEE-lee]. Clement's four-member team had won their school-level competition with a plan to address waste management in Kenya. Clement was reviewing his notes and trying to settle his jittered nerves. His team would present as the last of 57 teams at the 2015 regional competition in Dubai for a part of the coveted Hult Prize money to help launch their business idea. Clement stretched his restless body as much as he could in a sitting position. He thought about the great presentations he had heard. Did they have a chance?

---

[8] Clinton, Bill. "The Case for Optimism." 1 October 2012. *Time.* http://content.time.com/time/magazine/article/ 0,9171,2125031-1,00.html

Winners All

Team Taka Smart

Team Taka Smart didn't win at regionals, but you can't say they lost. They came back to campus and decided to launch their business idea anyway. They even garnered county support for it. Their business had designed a way to collect plastics assigning Taka points. People could collect Taka points and use the points to redeem for cell phone calling minutes.

Their business didn't change the world's waste problem, but it did make a difference. "Taka Smart is thriving," John Ngila reports today. "They have collected over 10,000 tons of plastics." The team has now turned to recycling, and hope to purchase a recycling machine in the near future.

Perhaps the most important change was in the team participants. Read their reactions in their own words:[9]

---

[9] Testimonials. *Africa Nazarene University* website.
    www.anu.ac.ke/testimonial

- "The Hult Prize Regionals gave us...a rare opportunity to be counted among world changers." – Jessica, Bachelor of Business Information Technology
- "I don't think the Hult Prize is just a competition but an effective driver to get young people thinking about world problems." Clement, Bachelor of Computer Science
- "We may not have won the Hult Prize Regionals, but we did leave...an African print on the hearts of everyone who was present." Saruni [sah-ROO-nee], Bachelor of Business Information Technology.
- In 2018 another team, KooKibanda[10] [koo-kee-BAHN-dah] represented ANU in Dubai with their idea to provide cold storage for fruits and vegetables in order to increase shelf life and reduce food waste. Their presentation won them a place at the six-week accelerator training at Ashridge Castle In London in September of the same year. This is the world's largest business accelerator. During this time, entrepreneurs receive coaching to fine-tune their business model, as well as gain access to "capital, mentorship, marketing, business development, customer acquisition, and talent recruitment."[11]

The benefits to the future of students who compete are enormous. The Hult Prize competition trains students to think about social entrepreneurship, gives them technical

---

[10] *Kibanda* means small hut, shack, or stall in Swahili.

[11] "Looking forward to attend the Hult-Business-Accelerator program at the Ashridge castle in London, England." Posted 11 May 2018. *Medium.* www.medium.com/@noormed.media/looking-forward-to-attend-the-hult-business-accelerator-program-at-the-ashridge-castle-in-london-163942fce26f

support with their projects, and encourages their networking with businesses that could help them in the future. Many participants have gone on to start their own businesses to address one of the many social issues in Kenya. You can be sure that ANU plans to continue their annual participation.

Campus Director Award

The team coaching impacted John Ngila as well. He was named one of the top ten campus directors of 2016 during the Hult Prize Regional Competition in Dubai. The honor came with admittance into a regional final of his choice, as well as admission into a number of prestigious conferences.

For John Ngila, the Hult competition was only a beginning. He hopes to start what he is initially calling a Social Entrepreneurship and Leadership Center. He is concerned that so much effort goes into the team competition and so many ideas take shape while only a few become viable launches. He wants an online depository "where all these businesses can be anchored, and we can come up with a way to support these ideas to become a reality." He received support from Microsoft, Dell, and a few other companies which have agreed to give IT support for the center. It's just another way to participate in transformation.

Simply Tools

Impact Week and the Hult Prize are simply tools. By themselves, they won't transform people or solve problems. However, when students understand that transformation is God's mission to the world; they become God's tools in an even bigger mission. They are refining their slingshots to use against their giants.

Nowhere is change more evident than in the field of technology. Its fast changing landscape may be a challenge for many, but it is another transformational tool at ANU and another story worth reading.

Chapter 4
Where Technology Transforms

Technology is a rising sun in Kenya. In fact, Kenya has become one of the leading African countries using and innovating with technology. This is true in spite of unemployment, poverty, and even with inadequate infrastructure for technology.[12] Africans began to call Kenya the Silicon Savannah beginning in 2007,[13] which spawned entrepreneurial interests that shows no signs of slowing down. ANU has had its hand on the pulse of this movement, especially because the school is located near Nairobi, considered the center of this technological expansion.

[12] Ndemo, Bitange, "How Kenya Became the Cradle of Africa's Technological Innovation." *Newsweek*. 27 December 2016. www.newsweek.com/how-kenya-became-cradle-africas-ict-innovation-534694

[13] Moime, Dipolelo. "Kenya, Africa's Silicon Valley, Epicentre of Innovation." *Venture Capital for Africa*. 25 April 2016. https://vc4a.com/blog/2016/04/25/kenya-africas-silicon-valley-epicentre-of-innovation.

The Amos Gichamba Story

Dr. Gichamba [gee-CHAHM-bah] wasn't thinking about technology as he grew up on a dairy farm in the central highlands of Kenya. He was thinking more about subsistence as he helped his family milk the cows and deliver the milk to the collection point as early as 4:00 a.m. on his way to school. It was even more difficult because his father worked at ANU during the week and only came home on weekends.

However, this ANU connection would serve Amos well. When Amos was ready to think about college, the ANU scholarship program for children of ANU employees made Africa Nazarene University his logical choice. Amos enrolled as a student in 2004. He chose computer science because he thought it offered him the best chance for employment.

Something transformational happened to Amos while at ANU which probably wouldn't have happened anywhere else. While his family had raised him Catholic with a belief in God, it had not translated into a personal relationship. "ANU provided a platform where I could take a deep reflection about my faith," he remembers. He joined the Christian Union Club, a student-led club that sponsored mission trips, worship teams, Bible studies, and other activities to influence spiritual growth. There he found people who expressed their faith fervently and acted on their beliefs. It made Amos examine his own beliefs more carefully.

> ANU provided a platform where I could take a deep reflection about my faith.

Eventually, Amos made a profession of personal faith in Jesus and began a new life as a born-again Christian. "I have learned to build my career as more of a servant and not pursue my own interests but actually to give back...I consult God in everything I do and want to be where He wants me to be," Amos testifies.

Especially with this new life change, Amos wanted to give back to the university. It is a theme that runs through the graduates who find more than education at ANU. "I had given myself three years to give back to the university," Amos explained, "...but after I came back; I realized that this was where I want to be."

Dr. Amos Gichamba

In 2007 when the department asked him to join them as an administrative assistant until he could complete his master's, Amos enthusiastically accepted. Amos began his master's program at Strathmore University in Nairobi because ANU did not offer a master's in business at that time. He also completed his Ph.D. there, as well. He gladly accepted a teaching position at his alma mater because he wanted to make it very clear "that as a graduate [of ANU], I wanted to come back." When the Department Chairman, Dr. Ngari [eeng-GAH-ree], left for South Africa for post-doctoral studies, Dr. Gichamba was made chairman of the Computer and Information Technology (CIT) Department.

While Dr. Gichamba no longer lives on his father's dairy farm, he didn't forget his rural roots. He created a cell phone app called M-Kulima [oom-koo-LEE-mah] for rural farmers. Amos remembered how his father was taken advantage of because he didn't have access to the going rate for selling dairy products. The M-Kulima app allowed a farmer to text a reputable database to receive the latest information on pricing. The Information and Communication Technology Authority of Kenya recognized his achievement with an award. *CNN Technology News* picked up the story as well.[14]

Today, the M-Kulima app is no longer in use, but Amos developed another platform while completing his Ph.D. at the University of Nairobi. It enables agricultural extension officers, agronomists, and development agencies supporting farmers to provide advisory services through text messages,

---

[14] Sutter, John D. "Mobile app developers tackle Africa's biggest problems." *CNN Technology News*. 12 April 2010. CNN. www.cnn.com/2010/TECH/04/12/africa.apps/index.html

a website, and a Multi-Lingual Interactive Voice Response system so the user can access agricultural information in Swahili and English.

Understanding how technology can offer solutions to problems in his country is the source of Dr. Gichamba's teaching passion. One of the new initiatives that he and his department are working on is an Innovation Center. It will be a web-based environment for incubating ideas through mentorship and collaboration. The department encourages students to use their class and research training to solve real-life problems with technology. It will be an open center where students from other universities can offer insights and improvements as well. Dr. Gichamba values inter-educational partnerships with alumni, research organizations, and ICT companies, both locally and internationally.

Boot Camp

Boot Camps offer an engaging way for the department to keep curriculum current. "The curriculum can be rigid because it is built on policies and procedures…so we support the curriculum with other activities," explains Dr. Gichamba. Boot Camp is an idea he experienced when he was working on his master's at Strathmore University in Nairobi. Boot Camps are intense workshop-based opportunities to learn new technology or to introduce trends in computing. It gives the department a chance to stay on the cutting edge. If Apple or Google releases a new mobile platform, for example, they don't have to wait to revise the curriculum; they simply offer a three-week workshop and teach it that way. "At the end of the day we are building a knowledge economy; we are building an innovative economy," says Dr. Gichamba.

Alumni Share in Transformation

The real reach of Africa Nazarene University lies in the alumni. As alumni graduate and connect their skills to their communities, they become transformational representatives for ANU. Dr. Gichamba keeps up with where their students find jobs. He is proud to report that you can find ANU CIT graduates in high-security positions in Kenya's Central Bank, as well as in the World Bank in Washington, D.C. Many alumni are entrepreneurs.

An example is Francis Kilemi [ke-LAY-mee], class of 2014. He hadn't even graduated when the Westgate Shopping Mall terrorist attack happened in Nairobi. It claimed 69 lives and wounded more than 170.[15] Francis went to social media and made a plea for blood donations before he stood in a long line of volunteers wishing to donate. Nothing about the blood donation process seemed as efficient as it could have been so Francis went to work to develop a better data-based partnership among hospitals and donors using the technology he had learned. "We see this as a problem that can be solved easily if all the hospitals, the government, and even the public can come together to share information," Francis reported. The result was Damu-Sasa[16]

---

[15] "Nairobi Westgate attack: Smoke rises at shopping complex." *BBC News*. 23 September 2018. BBC.
www.bbc.co.uk/news/world-africa-24199351

[16] *Damu-Sasa* website. www.damu-sasa.co.ke/welcome/index.php

[dah-moo-SAH-sah]. Translated from Swahili it means Blood-Now. In October 2018, a non-governmental agency, Amref Health Africa, and a technology solutions firm, Advanced IT Solutions (AISL), signed an agreement to use the Damu-Sasa blood management database system to track blood availability and location in order to improve patient access. This agreement followed a successful pilot program with the Kenyatta National Hospital, the largest referral hospital in East Africa.[17]

Francis was chosen to be part of the first Presidential Digital Talent Programme (PDTP) as an intern. He was one of 1,800 applicants from universities across the country. The PDTP is the Kenyan government's attempt to harness the brain power of young IT students who can help government agencies solve a conglomerate of public delivery systems.[18] Francis entered the competition because "Africa Nazarene University gave me a chance to attend workshop events, informative programs in organizations…and I felt that I was really well equipped to be one of the contenders."[19]

[17] Wanja, Claire. "Amref Kenya, Damu-Sasa Sign MoU to enhance blood services in Kenya." *Kenya Broadcasting Corporation*. 5 October 2018. www.kbc.co.ke/amref-kenya-damu-sasa-sign-mou-to-enhance-blood-services-in-kenya.

[18] Opportunities for Africans. "Government of Kenya Presidential Digital Talent Programme 2017/2018." Posted: 1 November 2017. *OpportunitiesForAfricans.com*. www.opportunitiesforafricans.com/government-of-kenya-presidential-digital-talent-programme-2018-for-kenyan-graduates.

[19] "Africa Nazarene University Alumni." *Africa Nazarene University* website. 23 March 2015. https://alumni2015.wordpress.com/?s=Francis.

Dr. Kendi Muchungi

Remember Dr. Muchungi and her research to develop a prototype for a retinal implant? She is another ANU graduate

Dr. Kendi Muchungi

using technology to transform. With the development of 3-D printing, computer science pairs with several disciplines in medical research. To understand the ground-breaking research she has been involved with, you have to understand how light must be converted into an electrical signal for visual perception to occur and for the brain to interpret it. The retina is an important part of this process. It is the light-sensitive layer of the eye which makes this light-to-brain signal transfer. When disease or injury breaks this retinal link, sight is impossible. Dr. Muchungi uses neuroscience to validate models for making a reconnection. It is research that opens the door to creating an artificial retinal implant one day.

Technological Transformation

Technology by itself doesn't transform. However, when students embrace the vision that "what begins here transforms the world," they begin to see the transformational power that rests in knowledge used in the right way. CIT student Ebuka [eh-BOO-kah] from Nigeria, believes that the ANU environment, as well as faculty and staff, empowered him in just this way. "I have been able to grow spiritually, physically and career-wise in ANU to unexplainable heights...ANU is the very best place to spread your wings and learn to fly with the support of both the faculty and staff."[20]

Dr. Gichambo and his competent team make transformation the purpose for technology. "My vision is to work together with my colleagues to build a research and innovation-oriented department, "Dr. Gichambo dreams. From mobile computing to computational neuroscience, the technological fields are endless. So is the transformation that they can accomplish. But it will take more than keystrokes; it will take people who make transformation their passion. It is the anthem that ANU continues to vocalize and students are learning it well.

But does ANU focus only on transformation in the areas of innovation and problem-solving to improve the quality of life in Africa? Certainly not. Their call to mission is rooted in the Great Commission. They are even more interested in sharing God's transforming work of the heart. However,

---

20 Henry, Ebuka. "Ebuka Henry (Nigeria)" *Africa Nazarene University* website. www.anu.ac.ke/testimonial/ebuka-henry-nigeria

with two campuses, students from twenty-six countries, tribal influences, and Spiritism roots; the mission is not easy. Since Chapel brings each campus together for this purpose, chapel offers the best overview of the opportunity for transformation.

Chapter 5
A Melting Pot for Mission

Students meander into the Helstrom Student Center where chapel will begin soon. Chapel becomes a melting pot of sorts as different cultures and traditions gather. It is where students will hear a careful articulation about spiritual transformation through Jesus as Chaplain Cindy North delivers the morning message. The prayer is that it will be an opening for the truth of God to find its way into hearts who may never have heard the gospel articulated in personal, passionate, and life-changing ways.

Cindy North has served ANU as director of Spiritual Development since 2014. Her husband, Rob, also serves at ANU as director of University Advancement. The Norths took positions at ANU after assignments at the Nazarene Theological College in South Africa and the Global Ministry Center in Lenexa, Kansas, USA. Cindy is an ordained elder in the Church of the Nazarene with a Doctor of Ministry degree from Asbury Theological Seminary with a passion for spiritual transformation.

Not a day goes by that her title and job description doesn't humble her. "I always feel overwhelmed but that calls me to my knees before the Lord where there are always answers and empowering beyond anything I can see or imagine," Cindy affirms.

How could anyone not be overwhelmed? Students come from more than twenty-six countries. On any year, the list can include Kenya, Tanzania, Uganda, Rwanda, Burundi, Malawi, Zimbabwe, Zambia, Sudan, Ethiopia, Eritrea, [er-uh-TREE-uh] to name a few. It is a patchwork of political, economic, social, family heritage and traditions that gather in classrooms, at basketball games, and in chapel.

The international element is one challenge. The fact that ANU is mostly a campus of commuters is another. Only four hundred students live in dormitories on the main campus while 1,500 commute to the main campus and 1,200 commute to the Nairobi campus. About half of the enrollment participates in evening classes.

Another challenge is the dual campus.

The City Campus
ANU's satellite campus is located at least a forty-five-minute drive to Nairobi when traffic congestion is low. It can take as long as two and one-half hours to make the one-way drive, depending on what time of day it is. The city

campus is in the densely populated central business district of Nairobi and has a different atmosphere.

ANU occupies part of the third floor and all top five floors of an eight-story building located at the traffic-congested area near the bus transportation terminal. A view from the top floor gives you a taste. A sidewalk market spills down one street while two people push a flatbed wagon piled high with bundles on a road crowded by taxis and cars. Pedestrians crisscross these busy streets without so much as a nod to any kind of traffic rules.

Day students are mostly post-secondary education students seeking a three-year diploma or a two-year certificate in various disciplines. While these are not university degrees, they are tickets into the workforce including placement in education, health, and business. Evening students are mostly engaged in a master's program and tend to be older and more focused.

ANU has also established distant learning centers that enroll students who are unable to travel to ANU's main or city campus. While managing students in so many different places makes connection difficult, it also enlarges the reach of the university.

Spiritual Development Team

Ministering to this rich diversity at ANU isn't easy. Cindy North works through a Spiritual Development Team. Shaun Bati [BAH-tee] is the full-time assistant chaplain for the main campus. He graduated in 2014 from ANU with a B.A. in Religion and is currently pursuing a master's in religion at ANU. Pastor Charles Onyango [ohn-YAHNG-goh] is the full-time assistant chaplain for the Town Campus. He is an ordained elder also serving as associate pastor for the Riuru [ree-OO-roo] Church of the Nazarene thirty minutes outside of Nairobi. Veronica Mutaganswa [moo-tah-GAHN-swah] is the administrative assistant in the Chaplain's office. She does more than secretarial work. She often prays with students and is involved in discipleship activities among the students. The Spiritual Development Team supervise chapels and strengthen a discipleship focus among students. They also plan Holiness Week.

Holiness Week is a focused, five-day spiritual emphasis that occurs the first month of each of the trimesters that constitute the academic year. The Spiritual Development Team invites a special speaker that fits the student population and context, someone who can articulate and engage. The first week takes place on the main campus and the second week moves to the city campus in Nairobi. With music, prayer, message, and an invitation to personally accept Christ's invitation to follow Him; Holiness Week is the transformational call to make following God a life-long pursuit. "You are an agent of change," Rev. Mashangu [mah-SHAHNG-goo] Maluleka [mah-loo-LAY-kah][21] proclaimed during Holiness Week 2016. "You are God's transforming power that is supposed to move and shake Africa." But this isn't just a call

---

[21] Rev. Mashangu Maluleka passed away suddenly on 6 January 2018. He had served as field strategy coordinator for Africa South, as well as pastor of the Divine Hope Church of the Nazarene, Pretoria, South Africa. To learn more about Maluleka, visit here: www.nazarene.org/article/field-strategy-coordinator-mashangu-maluleka-passes-away

The student worship team for Town Campus
sings from their heart.

to social action. This is a clear invitation to give God first authority in transformation.

It is a beautiful sight to see students praying at the front altars. Some recommit their lives to Christ. Some experience a spiritual breakthrough. Some come to Christ for the first time. As you think of ANU, pray for these critical encounters and the people who are changed because of them. Answers to prayer here are a major priority for ANU.

Addressing Other World Religions

Another challenge ANU faces has to do with students with different religious backgrounds. The same national law that made a private Christian university possible is the same law that gives other world religions the right to practice their faith. However, the Student Handbook clearly states that "ANU is purely a Christian university and therefore only provides places of worship for Christians. Students of any other religion are expected to make their own private arrangements outside of the university premises." The good news is that the law doesn't interfere with the school's authority to require chapel attendance of all students.

Both campuses have chapel. The main campus holds chapel on Tuesdays and Thursdays. The town campus has an hour chapel Mondays and Wednesdays, as well as a forty-five-minute evening chapel which rotates days Monday through Thursday. The reason for the rotations is in order not to interrupt the same class. However, a routine class and chapel schedule can't work around required prayer rituals. Some students must leave class and often the building to keep these prayer times.

Of course, not every student considers chapel important. A student who attended classes at the city campus had been missing chapel, so the Chaplain's office contacted the student's mother. The family fell into the twenty percent of Kenyans who were not Christian.[22] The mother was very unhappy hearing that her son was missing the good teaching from chapel and promised she would make sure her son was back in chapel. Religious differences weren't as important to this mother as getting "good teaching."

Also, there is fear from students from different religious backgrounds about showing any open agreement with the

[22] "Kenya." *The World Factbook*. See "Religions" in "Population" section. www.cia.gov/library/publications/the-world-factbook/geos/ke.html

Christian message. It is a challenge about which the whole Spiritual Development Team continues to pray. Take, for example, one young woman who stayed in her seat one morning at the end of chapel when everyone left the room.

"Would you like someone to pray with you?" the prayer counselor asked.

"I can't be seen praying here," the student replied, keeping her head down.

When Chaplain North learned what happened, she sighed. She understood the Implications the girl faced. Her family could disown her or worse. But God heard her heart and if staying in her seat was her way of showing interest, it was an opening. There are "many opportunities on the front line," Cindy North thought. After all, opportunity is the raw material for transformation.

> **There are many opportunities on the front line.**

Mission Trips

One key way to help students catch the vision for participating in spiritual transformation involves mission trips. Mission trips give students a chance to engage in compassionate ministry. Most of the time, they don't have to go very far to do it. The annual mission trip to work with the Mathare [maht-HAH-ray] Church of the Nazarene, and the school they administrate in this poverty-stricken area, is only one example.

To call Mathare a slum is almost an understatement. It looks more like a trash heap. It is a forgotten plain of patchwork sheds where you think nothing human could possibly live. But they do. Families claim 6' x 8' (1.8 m x 2.4 m) tin rectangles, patch them with mud and call them home. Nearly 500,000 people live on this scarred terrain of only three square miles (7.7 square kilometers).[23]

ANU is taking their mission of transformation to this uncomfortable place.[24] The Christian Union Club, a student-led club that provides ministry opportunities across Kenya in high schools, colleges, and universities, has an active group at ANU. They try to plan at least one outreach trip to Mathare a year. The gift of the "Glory Bus" in 2016 by an anonymous donor makes the trip through Nairobi possible. The team wants to bring childhood back to children who know little except survival by crime or drugs. With ANU volunteers, they play games, enjoy simple art, and share Bible stories. The team also connects with teenagers to address critical adolescent issues in light of the high prevalence of HIV/AIDS. Paris Akoyi [ah-KOH-yay], a graduate of ANU, heads the Community Care School that her father, Rev. Paul Akoyi started. Other groups on campus have stepped up to participate in this outreach.

The Garissa University Response

ANU students also look for other ways to reach out. When terrorists attacked the Kenyan campus of Garissa

---

[23] "Mathare Valley." *Wikipedia.*
https://en.wikipedia.org/wiki/Mathare_Valley

[24] Crofford, Amy. "A channel for God's blessing." *Engage* Magazine. 22 September 2016.
www.engagemagazine.com/content/channel-gods-blessing

[guh-RIS-suh] University College, they killed 148 people, most of them singled-out as Christian. Even though Garissa is located 230 miles northeast of Nairobi, ANU considered this tragedy one they should address. They responded tangibly by gathering food and drinks and delivering them to the Red Cross who would distribute them to huddled families waiting for identification of a family member.

They also gathered in another way. They gathered to pray. "In the aftermath of the Garissa attack, our ANU community…provided a quiet place to pray over the many issues and concerns this event has brought to everyone in Kenya," Chaplain North explained.

Although the Spiritual Development Team is committed to providing as many avenues as possible for students to encounter their need for spiritual transformation, sometimes God just leads a person into the right place at the right time. That's Enok's story of transformation.

Enok's Story

Enok is an example of a life transformed. His parents separated seven months after he was born, and the court sent baby Enok to live with his father. After his father died when Enok was six years old, Enok endured a long series of unpredictable and often dangerous places to live. More than once his very life was in jeopardy. More than once he lived isolated and barely surviving.

It wasn't until he was thrown out of a temporary home with nothing but the clothes he had, that he providentially connected to someone who not only gave him a room, but a job as well. For the first time, Enok realized that there was an unseen force protecting him. He believed it was God and decided to go to a nearby church on Sunday. If God really was watching out for him, perhaps he should get to know this God better.

He was in high school when a visitor to his school met Enok and was especially interested in Enok's story. In fact, he was so moved by the courage and tenacity of Enok, he decided to sponsor the rest of his education including college.

Enok heard about Africa Nazarene University from a friend. Even though he didn't know anything about Nazarene, he decided to check it out. As soon as he enrolled, he confronted a world of belonging he had heard about but never experienced.

"Life at Africa Nazarene has been beautiful…Through community, I got to know Dr. Cindy. She has been my spiritual mother…[and] that has also enhanced my relationship with God…My vision has been to be a voice for the voiceless in my society."

In a very real way, life began for Enok at ANU. It's where he found his call from God to share his transformed life with others.

This is the prayer on the hearts of faculty, staff, and administration when they gather for chapel. They want to see more like Enok finding their way through complicated circumstances all the way to God. They want to see transformation that begins in the heart.

Back to Chapel

Let's peek in as students gather for chapel to start on the eighth floor of the city campus. The worship team has finished their practice and is ready. There is just one more thing they need to do. They need to pray. The student leader of the worship team gathers the vocalists and instrumentalists in a circle. They hold hands and pray that God would take them past their practice and open hearts through music and through the words of the speaker.

Chaplain North smiles. "Yes," she agreed. "This is the way to transformation."

While spiritual transformation is the cornerstone of ANU and students are their primary target, the university has a reach into the surrounding community as well. On a continent where the land needs a different kind of transformation, ANU is taking the message there, too. And a graduate of ANU, John Henry, has become their spokesperson.

Chapter 6

Transforming the Land *and* People

John Henry Ogonda [oh-GAHN-dah] stood in the center of school children, their parents, and teachers, with shovel in hand.

"See. This is how you dig to plant beans."

John Henry had chosen a hillside slope and dug out a shelf to create a two-level terrace.

"This will preserve the water that comes," he explained. "Now you," he said and motioned to a few to pick up their shovels. This is the way they become initiates into dryland farming just like John Henry learned it as a child.

John Henry's Story

For a moment, John Henry could hear his mother's voice. She had been his first teacher of the land as he was growing up in western Kenya. Farming there was always a war against drought, overused soil, and unrelenting heat. But his mother had learned to let the land be her teacher. She learned what protected vulnerable seedlings. She did not replant what struggled to grow without good results. Water was scarce, and his mother found inventive ways to conserve it. She taught John Henry to listen to the land as it protested or sang. John Henry became one of those seedlings, growing in a dry land, and surviving. His survival became a call to work the land, protect it, restore it, and teach others to do the same.

By the time John Henry was ready for high school, he had to study business because the Kenyan government had removed agriculture from its curriculum. However, when his high school business teacher started a farm club to generate food for the school, John Henry found his sweet spot. What she meant as a business lesson, John Henry used to fuel his passion: learn the land and make it your friend. The club project taught him new ways to get water. They used clean waste water from the kitchen to recycle for the land.

Coming to ANU

When it was time to consider college, John Henry's sister offered to help him find a university in Nairobi because that's where she lived. Among the brochures she collected was one from Africa Nazarene University. John Henry was pleased to discover that they offered a degree in natural science. He also was intrigued by the campus itself. The university was a garden in the middle of dry land. What a wonderful place to find out how somebody could make land bloom.

But how would a mshamba [muh-SHAHM-bah], a primitive farm boy, fit in with all the flashy students who had come from cities? Not very well at first. He sat on the sidelines without mixing with the other students during orientation days. Nothing changed until he met Vice-Cancellor Marangu. She found John Henry sitting by himself as usual. She startled him into a reality he hadn't thought about when she said,

> Your graduation date is set, and the countdown starts now. You have to start with the end in mind, and you have to be responsible. There will be no bells to wake you up, no one to tell you to go eat, do assignments, [or] read.

That's when John Henry knew she had been sent as his guardian angel. He couldn't let his insecurity keep him from diving into his university experience.

It wasn't until John Henry joined the Environmental Club to participate in planting on campus that he met the vice-chancellor in a way that influenced the rest of his time on campus. He couldn't believe that she was planting with them, shoulder to shoulder, shovel to shovel. That day John Henry learned that she was "the V.C. who makes her hands dirty for the betterment of the workplace."

Few of his peers understood why John Henry was so serious about soil and plants. They had mostly negative perceptions about farming. Poor people farmed. Retired people farmed. The future was in computers and technology.

It didn't faze John Henry. The very fact they had such thoughts about the land and farming just made him more determined to show them something different. "I want to do something that will make people productive, something I can use to be employed and that will employ others," John Henry would explain.

In 2013 John Henry graduated with his degree from ANU. Vice-Chancellor Marangu recognized they had a colleague in John Henry. The university asked him to stay on as assistant administrator in the Department of Environment and Natural Resource. He joined the staff in a mission of transformation. While the land needed much transformation, there would be no change unless he could bring transformation to people as well.

And that's why he was at a local school training students and their parents about dryland farming. "What I do [comes] from my experience with [lack of] water at home, and I don't want others to go through the negative side."

John Henry loves to plant!

Dryland Farming

As a student, John Henry learned much about the Maasai people whose land borders the ANU campus. He understood that Maasai know cattle better than crops. John Henry is introducing dryland farming to Kenyan Maasai people in order to double their ability to feed their families. The same land can produce twenty times more in crops for nourishment than what the cows can produce to feed a family. He teaches the Maasai to plant tomatoes, watermelon, and their traditional beans. He tells them that by following his care plan, they can start harvesting in just five weeks! That's a lot less time than it takes to raise a cow for market or slaughter.

John Henry is a teacher in these moments. He won't come to their school unless he can teach parents *and* children because he knows the importance of owning the lessons. They must dig the soil, plant the seeds, and water for themselves. If the plant fails for lack of care, they must feel the lost opportunity and the missing meal.

A Transformational Vision

He also has a transformational vision for the students at ANU. Many students have little background in agriculture. They have come from cities and buy their food at groceries or markets. John Henry always tries to take a student with him to observe when he teaches dryland planting.

If you talk to John Henry enough, you will hear him repeat his favorite saying: "If you're not part of the solution, you're part of the problem." John Henry is always looking to be part of the solution and wants to involve others. "Use what you have [and] be the change you want to see." He read this from Dr. Isaac Kalua [kah-LOO-uh], one of John Henry's contemporary influencers. Dr. Kalua founded the Green Africa Foundation[25] in 2000. The Foundation's purpose was to get Kenyans to take care of the land and plant more trees and reduce deforestation.

When John Henry invited renowned Kenyan environmentalist, Dr. Kalua, to speak for the Environmental Club, and everyone was surprised that he accepted.[26] John Henry had created the "Plant Your Stay, Save the Earth" campaign to increase campus participation in greening up their part of the world. The campaign encouraged staff to plant a tree for each year of service at ANU while students planted trees to equal three times the number of semesters remaining before graduation. Dr. Kalua's Foundation donated 2,000 seedlings for the event.

The Green Culture Movement for ANU

John Henry wants ANU students to participate in their own green initiative. That's why he started The Green Culture Movement. "The moment you touch the environment you affect the climate and wildlife" he explains. "You cannot separate farming and the environment." He knows that repeated habits become part of the culture. He wants

---

[25] *Green Africa Foundation* website. www.greenafricafoundation.org

[26] Kalua, Isaac. "One Car One Dollar Tree Project." *Green Africa Foundation*. 3 December 2013. www.autoterminal.co.jp/web/download/One_car_one_dollar_report_12_March_2013.pdf.

the culture of the ANU campus to think green and do green and "be the solution."

John Henry leads by example. He plants a tree when there is something to celebrate. He believes that a tree is something that will grow and add more than a memory or historical review. He celebrates a birthday by bringing a seedling to plant. He honors a life that has ended by planting a tree in memory. When someone opens a building, or starts an organization, they need a tree and John Henry brings one.

A Servant at Heart

John Henry is making a difference at ANU and in his larger community. His gentle, soft-spoken, understated determination does not go unnoticed. A local station in terviewed him. Schools request his help. He's taken up his mentor's ways and is the one "who makes [his] hands dirty." He's even working on a book to identify every plant and tree on the campus of ANU. He's asked faculty member Amy Crofford, who doesn't go anywhere without her camera, to take pictures for the project. He has finished around twenty-five botanical varieties and has about thirty to go. Students are redoing the identification tags that are beginning to show their age. It is his love for the school that gives him a chance to do what he loves.

> He wants the culture of the ANU campus to think green and do green and "be the solution."

Some believe that buildings make the biggest difference as they raise their walls above the land. John Henry borrows the vision of his mentor, Professor Marangu, as he shares that the land is a living illustration about what God wants to do with a life. He believes that God wants the beauty of the land to remind students and everyone else that God brings beauty to a life He transforms. John Henry believes it because it happened to him!

Chapter 7
Empowering Pastors

Another part of the transformational mission of ANU involves empowering pastors. ANU has a dedicated team of religion and Christian ministry faculty who want the good news of God to impact their students in such a way that sharing the gospel becomes their purpose and passion.

The task is daunting: prepare pastors and ministry servants for their unevenly developing continent. At present, there are over 150 graduates from the bachelor's program and another fifty from the master's program. They serve not only in Kenya, but in Nigeria, Côte d'Ivoire [KOHT di-VWAHR], Ghana, Ethiopia, the Democratic Republic of the Congo, Rwanda, Zambia, Zimbabwe, and Uganda.

While every student's story is a story of challenge, call, and transformation, the story of Rev. Joseph Kisoi [kee-SOY-ee], is a good one to share. He has found his place in the transformational mission as part of the faculty in the School of Religion and Christian Ministry, (SRCM). As part of the third graduating class of ANU, he has seen a lot of transformation.

Once you hear the resonant, bass voice of Kenyan, Joseph Kisoi, you don't forget it. Or maybe it is the way his smile puts you at ease and treats you like a welcomed friend. He is engaging, articulate, and passionate about ANU. He has taught here since 2001. In fact, once he came as a student to ANU in 1997, he never left.

He is one of six full-time and ten part-time lecturers that complete the school's teaching faculty for more than one hundred students enrolled in classes. He became the first African to be employed full-time in the School of Religion and Christian Ministry.

Rev. Joseph Kisoi, School of Religion and Christian Ministry

To say ANU has been a transformational part of his life is an understatement. He met his wife at the school, worked in the Dean of Students Office after graduating, raised his family of three daughters here, and finished a Master of Religion here.

Joseph grew up in a family of six in Kangundo [kahn-GOON-doh], the ninth largest urban area in Kenya. He remembers how coming to ANU in the early days was like coming to an outpost in the middle of a wildlife reserve.

The giraffes would come and eat from the trees. My wife and I met lions at very close range three times. Once we were seated about 100 meters (109 yards) outside the university and right where we were seated a lion sat in the bushes. The second time we met one on the road, but fortunately we were driving. The third time we met lions at our gate when we were trying to drive in.

We also had zebras coming around here. We had hippos about 200 meters (218 yards) from the university.

Of course, the scene is different today. The fenced property restricts animal access. Only the monkeys that live in the cliffs on the other side of the Athi River that backs the campus can still wander through occasionally.

When Joseph arrived at ANU, he had never heard of the Church of the Nazarene.

I didn't know there was any denomination known as Church of the Nazarene. So, I came here and came to know Nazarenes and what they stand for, and I

A giraffe meanders behind the campus in the early days.

fell in love with the Church of the Nazarene. That's when I resolved to become a minister in the Church of the Nazarene.

Joseph remembers a barren campus. There was a chapel, dormitories, and the religion department with six students, including himself. He has seen great growth in student and faculty population, campus aesthetics, number of buildings, and the way ANU is empowering and sending pastors.

Passing on the message of holiness to a new generation of pastors for Africa is the passion of this godly man. He is in tune with the challenges his students face, because he grew up with them.

There are many challenges in articulating the holiness message to African pastors. One is cultural barriers. Whenever there is a crisis, many of our people seem to resort back to heathen ways. They want to know and witness the power of God [but] it's like a door that seems so tall within Africa, where the power of God is on one side, and the power of darkness fighting almost equally on the other side.

I think the challenge raises the need for discipleship. People need to be discipled to maturity in Christ, and to know how to disentangle themselves from worldliness.

The other challenge is environment. We don't seem to link our theology to our environment. The Bible connects it and sets humans in the Garden to have a relationship with the Holy Other. I see the need of an ecological theology, an ecological hermeneutic.

The other challenge has to do with money. For the last three years, I have not seen many rains. A huge percentage of the African people are agricultural. They have suffered economically because of the drought. For people who work in offices, they may not notice the impact of the drought. But for the poor farmer, it is a big challenge. I see that as a challenge; because when you minister to starving people and speak of the goodness of God in the midst of all these crises, you have people asking how is there the good Lord who loves and cares for us and who does not send rain.

While these questions are complicated to address, they provide ways for pastors to reach people where they are. Empowering pastors to deal with these and other issues becomes more than a curriculum decision, it becomes a mandate.

Engaging students with real issues and opening them to the power of God is his mission, is Rev. Kisoi's passion.

Nothing encourages him more than to see transformation in a student's life.

> I teach Old Testament. Occasionally I will have students come…who don't profess to know Christ. Sometimes one comes to my office and will say "Professor, because of what I learned, I want to surrender my life to the Lord Jesus Christ." That is most rewarding.

> Other times a student, even from other departments, will come and say "I want to do a minor in theology." That is encouraging that people sense the value in theological education.

It isn't easy to be a pastor in Africa. There are family expectations and cultural perceptions that can send a religion major on an uphill journey. Rev. Kisoi explains:

> Here in Africa, the concept of being a pastor is looked down upon. They say "as quiet as a church mouse, as dry as a pastor's throat, as empty as a pastor's pocket." People don't think you can have meaningful employment after studying theology. Many of our students who come to study theology are sort of abandoned by their families. People would be willing to sell property to help a student take computer science or commerce. Not many would do it for a student in theology. That's why many of our students who study theology are sponsored by the churches from which they come.

While ANU helps students with scholarships, they are never enough. But Joseph Kisoi isn't discouraged.

I would say as a church we are in a very strategic position to spread the holiness message. We see a lot of transformation here. I believe it is our Wesleyan Holiness background that has something to offer to the rest of the world because it is a rare message.

From the six students that Joseph was a part of when he began attending ANU, there are now a hundred students or more. Most will become pastors, while some will become teachers in theological institutions, and others will take positions in faith-based parachurch organizations.

Training these students does not come only from books and lectures. Students are required to intern at local churches. Nazarene African pastors provide much-needed mentoring. Some students find real-life learning as they assist in the Chaplain's office, lead worship services, or conduct Bible studies. Twice a year, the Religion Student Association (RSA) hosts a mission outreach to villages in Kenya. They hold revival services or show the JESUS Film, whatever will call people to salvation or strengthen faith. This is real-time application for students, and they take it very seriously.

> I would say as a church we are in a very strategic position to spread the holiness message.

Rev. Kisoi is part of a great story at ANU, a great transformation. He joins every resident or visiting lecturer in empowering students who will preach and teach and have a transformational impact on others. Two of those students are now teaching at ANU in the School of Religion. Rev. Kisoi points to their offices and smiles.

Dr. Kamau [kah-MAW-oo] was my student. Gift Mtukwa [em-TOO-kwah] was my student, now head of this department. So yes, I have been part of the story, and it is good. I can only say that everybody has a small corner assigned by God in which to share the light of God. I believe we are doing our best to be sure we are the light of Christ where we are!

Empowering pastors to take their corner of this daunting task is only part of ANU's goal. Students in other departments have a corner of responsibility as well. They will be lawyers, judges, teachers, news reporters, business developers to name just a few. While there isn't room to tell all of the stories, a few examples will help you see the potential reach that ANU has into the culture.

Chapter 8
Transforming the Culture

Transformed people transform the world, not by ideologies or charisma or notoriety. Real transformation takes place when students take what they've learned and put it into practice. By now you understand that it is not just one school or department or administrator who articulates the message of transformation at ANU. It is pervasive throughout classes, clubs, lectures, workshop, emails, and special emphases.

One place where academics meet the culture is through the Law School.

The Law School

In 2010 ANU opened the Law School. The university received accreditation for the school in 2014. In fact, ANU is "the first university to receive full five-year accreditation from the Council for Legal Education in Kenya. This is the maximum allowable. It shows the confidence they're placing in us," Deputy Vice-Chancellor Rod Reed says with understandable pride.

Why would a relatively small liberal arts school tackle something as complicated as law in the middle of a country known for its corruption? To John, a recent graduate, it is because "Africa Nazarene University Law School (ANULS) made me the lawyer that the world was yearning for—a selfless lawyer full of integrity and concerned to serve humanity."[27]

Most of the law students credit their participation in Moot Court Competitions as critical preparation for legal processes they face after graduation. This is a competition that simulates the court setting to give law students a chance to argue cases in as-real-as-possible situations. It is a judged competition where they select a winning team, as well as awarding prizes for excellence in individual presentations.

> Africa Nazarene University Law School (ANULS) made me the lawyer that the world was yearning for—a selfless lawyer full of integrity and concerned to serve humanity.

ANU has participated regularly in Moot Court Competitions, both nationally and internationally, and often come back with awards. They have brought home awards for Best Oralist, Most Promising Advocate, Best Kenyan Speaker, and Best Speaker. They have hosted their

---

[27] Testimonials. *Africa Nazarene University* website. www.anu.ac.ke/testimonial

third Annual Foreign Direct Investment Moot Court competition. This Moot Court addresses the legal issues that involve international treaties, as well as disputes.

In the Moot Court Competition at Bharati [ba-RAH-tee] Vidyapeeth [veed-YAH-peth] Deemed [DEEMD] University in India, ANU's three-person team placed second out of 33 teams in March 2018. Over the course of their involvement in these competitions, students have presented arguments in simulated courts about human rights, children's advocacy, amnesty, and other issues that plague their country and the world. It is a stellar accomplishment for such a new law school!

Law students aren't waiting for graduation to make a difference. They organized their own Law School Journal that is "the only internationally acclaimed law journal published by a law school in Kenya."[28] Law students research international and comparative law focusing on African legal issues. International lawyers are paying attention!

Law students receive their award at the Moot Court Competition, Bahrati, India

---

[28] Mwangi-Okwemba, Wambui. "ANU Hosts Africa's First Regional Foreign Direct Investment Moot Court Competition." *Aspire.* October 2016, Issue 400, p. 29.

Within the Law School is the Department of Peace and Conflict. Through classes and workshops, this department also has an important reach.

The Department of Peace and Conflict

In this country of tribal conflict and border disputes, attempting to mitigate generational conflict is no small matter. Classes in this department share Christian ethics without apology. Imagine how significant it is that generals from Kenya's military, the national spokesperson for the Kenya police force, as well as senators and members of Parliament, have passed through ANU programs and graduated. The Peace and Conflict classes have especially caught the attention of civic and political leaders. Some have even studied for master's degrees at ANU. "We think that a lot of our programs are really making a difference in society. That's so rewarding to see that people of substance are coming to be part of your programs," Deputy Vice-Chancellor Rod Reed expressed.

One of those graduates making a difference is Beatrice Elachi [e-LAH-tee]. She was nominated to the Kenya Senate in 2013 and became the Majority Whip, the first woman to hold that position in Kenya's Parliament. In 2017 she became Speaker of the Nairobi County Assembly. Her bachelor and master's degrees in Governance, Peace, and Security Studies from ANU have served her well on the front lines of many conflicts, including a very personal one that brought intense opposition and scrutiny and was sourced in corruption. Pray for Beatrice Elachi as she awaits legal resolution from the courts.

Influencers like Beatrice Elachi are those who find the best way to communicate messages that inspire, warn, and innovate. Another department that focuses on ways to make this happen is the Department of Mass Communication.

The Department of Mass Communication

ANU's Department of Mass Communication trains influencers in broadcasting, journalism, public relations, and graphic design. Their state-of-the-art radio and television studios help them accomplish this goal. The fourth floor of the town campus building in Nairobi houses the rooms where students learn and practice the different components of mass communication. While one room is practicing a news presentation, another room is filled with students editing their films, and still another finds students glued to computer screens designing magazine layouts.

In the TV production studio

The transformational story of ANU would not be complete without sharing a couple more stories of graduates who have garnered positive notoriety in Kenya.

A Computer Science Graduate Turned Broadcaster

Waihiga [wee-HEE-gah] Mwaura [em-WAH-rah] graduated from ANU with a degree in computer science, but he has turned to broadcast journalism in an award-winning way. He found his sweet spot in sports broadcasting. CNN honored his work with the MultiChoice award for African journalists in 2012 for a story on a team of Maasai warriors training for cricket while learning about preventing HIV/AIDS. Most recently he won the BBC World News *Komla* [KOHM-lah] Dumor [DOO-mohr] award for his ability to give Africans a voice through his storytelling and investigative reporting.[29]

Waihiga is known for his playful spirit, investigative journalism, and Christian witness. When interviewed on KBC TV, the state-run television station that broadcasts news, entertainment, and educational programming; Waihiga began the interview by saying, "I believe in a good God who allows us to go through hard times but ultimately takes care of us."[30] He explained that "What drives me is impacting the world, and as a Christian, I am

[29] "Kenyan Waihiga Mwaura wins BBC World News Komla Dumor award." *BBC.com.* 26 September 2018. www.bbc.com/news/world-africa-45573691

[30] "Beyond the Screen S01E07 Waihiga Mwaura." *W TV Kenya.* 24 November 2015. www.youtube.com/watch?v=5QNw_qS6ta4

compassionate [about] world issues and I believe in…what God has planned for me."[31]

A Banker Turned Innovative Entrepreneur

Lorna Rutto [ROO-toh] also graduated from ANU. However, she found using her accounting degree in banking to be unfulfilling. That's when she branched out into an entrepreneurial start-up that changed her life and is headed to change the lives of others. Her business uses trashed plastics redeemed from dumpsites and garbage cans to manufacture fence posts. Named EcoPost, it has become a $150,000 business that employs more than 500. In 2011, she won a Cartier Women's Initiative Award for her successful business to address an environmental issue.[32] Every month her company re-purposes twenty tons of plastic waste to save over 250 acres of trees.[33] Her vision is *To Transform Africa's Waste into Wealth*, and she's doing it one fence post at a time.

Law students, journalists, broadcasters, entrepreneurs—they are transformers. You see it in their eyes. You hear it in their goals. You recognize it as they experiment with engaging their culture.

---

[31] "Waihiga Mwaura Profile," *Kenyan Life*.
www.kenyanlife.info/waihiga-mwaura

[32] "Laureate 2011 Sub-Saharan Africa: Lorna Rutto." *Cartier Women's Initiative Awards*.
www.cartierwomensinitiative.com/candidate/lorna-rutto

[33] Iwuoha, John-Paul. "Lorna Rutto – The innovative entrepreneur who creates wealth and jobs from plastic waste." *Smallstarter*. Posted: 16 June 2013. www.smallstarter.com/get-inspired/lorna-rutto

Remember, ANU wouldn't have happened without you, your prayers, your giving, and your volunteering. You are a part of a global partnership. It's a reminder we all need.

Chapter 9
A Global Partnership

How do you tell the story of a global partnership? It is a story of more than the missionaries we send. It is a story that Work & Witness, Faith Promise, and prayer from Nazarenes around the world makes possible.

John Opiyo [oh-PEE-yoh] knows this firsthand. He has been the finance director since 2014 for ANU. He's been a part of the ANU story since graduating with the first class in 1994. He joined the Church of the Nazarene with his parents when the denomination first came into Kenya in 1985. ANU has given him a career and a calling for which he is grateful.

John readily acknowledges that ANU is not an institution on its own. The partnership between the Church of the Nazarene and the institution is a major part of the school's success. This is the way he says it:

If you talk about ANU resources, you cannot leave the Church of the Nazarene out. The general church has given significantly to the university in terms of teams coming to support the infrastructure, or people coming to teach, or missionaries. That helped us to keep our fees at a reasonable level so that more students are able to afford our education.

Ask John Opiyo why he would recommend African Nazarene University and he has a very specific response.

It's not just about competence. There's more to education here than just a grade. We give students a package. We develop the whole person. I've seen it. A student comes with difficulties or habits, and they give their life to God or their life has changed in some way, is transformed.

> A student comes with difficulties or habits, and they give their life to God or their life has changed in some way, is transformed.

I would tell students about our quality of education. I would tell them about the values I hope they leave here with. And if they desire employment, we have a good name among businesses.

John is proud to be a part of a school that makes such a difference. He is grateful to the Church of the Nazarene for their partnership.

Few initiatives say "partnership" better than Work & Witness. ANU has a long love relationship with Work & Witness teams because they have had a major role in the development of the university. While not everyone can take a Work & Witness trip, everyone can celebrate what happens when people do.

Work & Witness at ANU

Work & Witness is so important to the DNA of ANU that they built an Honors Court in the middle of the campus to recognize those who gave their time, energy, and skill to transform some part of the campus. At the clock tower in the center of the campus, shoulder-high walls of mortared bricks and cement blocks spoke in eight directions. Each wall bears the engraved plaques that record the individual

The October, 2017 IT team at the unveiling of their plaque for the Honors Court.

names of those who came with Work & Witness teams and the year they volunteered. The first plaque identifies a team from Pasadena, California, USA, in 1988.

However, not all projects at a university are the typical Work & Witness projects.

Cataloguing 50,000 Books!

The formidable wall of more than 590 boxes of donated books from the Nazarene Bible College is one of these projects. The books must be catalogued before students and faculty can use them. In 2018, five librarians joined an IT Work & Witness team to help the Grace Roles Library staff. They were able to train the ANU staff on the new library system available for use at all Nazarene higher education institutions. This allows ANU cataloguers to access records for the Nazarene Bible College books. It has the potential of reducing cataloguing time significantly.

Faculty and staff stand in front of the boxes of donated books from Nazarene Bible College.

Sharing IT Skills

Another specialized Work & Witness team involves using IT skills. Josh Williams heads this initiative for the global church. Most recently he led two teams to ANU, made up of individuals with a variety of IT and engineering skills from different areas of the United States. They arrived on campus with pre-purchased security cameras and equipment. They have successfully installed more than 120 security cameras between the two campuses. This addresses a much-needed security enhancement to comply with the Kenyan Department of Education's security requirements for all Kenyan universities. Plans are developing to return and continue their work on the security system, as well as help install updated technology for classrooms, including biometric cameras to register class attendance.

There are other ways to join the global partnership, and you don't have to quit your job and move to ANU to make a difference. You can make a difference where you are by praying.

How You Can Pray

Robert wants to be a judge. He knows that he will need the help of God to achieve this goal. He recognizes that he must know and represent the laws of man and government. However, he wants to be more than a *good* judge; he wants to be a *godly* judge. Pray for Robert and others like him in the Law School.

Faith is a beautiful girl with a beautiful name. She is studying mass communication and wants to go into news broadcasting. News will keep her in the places where people are in crisis, and she can speak the compassion of God there. Pray for Faith and other students studying communication, that they will also understand their role as spokespersons for God.

Maria has cerebral palsy. However, you don't see it in her brilliant, illuminating smile. She "accidentally" found

ANU when searching for a college that would accept her. Maria found more than education at ANU; she found her life calling. "I can now speak for the children that have cerebral palsy and open doors for them. It is amazing what the world says is impossible, and what the world says is not good enough, is the one God uses to do His work and bring hope." Pray for Maria and others who find out what they *can* do instead of what they can't and use it to make a difference.

Pray for every faculty member mentioned and those who were not. Pray for new ways to reach students with the timeless message of God's redemption and empowerment. Pray for the conferences and workshops that bring many people to the campus.

Pray for an eternal imprint that goes past innovation, technology, or human success.

Pray for the future of ANU as the university faces something they haven't faced in twenty-one years. With the retirement of Professor Leah T. Marangu, the Board of Trustees has selected a new vice-chancellor, Dr. Stanley Makhosi [mah-KOH-see] Bhebhe [BE-bay]. His story is also a story of transformation that reminds us how God works over time to raise up new leaders.

Chapter 10

For a New Future

Dr. Stanley Bhebhe stands in front of the backdrop of red and gold curtains, colors that symbolize the vibrancy of Africa Nazarene University, as he waits to be inaugurated as the third vice-chancellor of this twenty-five year-old university. The festivities are happening in the Helstrom Student Centre, a building that exists as tangible result of multiple Work & Witness groups. Dr. Bhebhe is surrounded by ANU colleagues, students, friends, and dignitaries from Africa and North America.

It is hard for him not to review the journey that brought him here. He thinks about his father, mostly raised by Salvation Army missionaries who stepped in when his mother died. They were his father's early mentors and nurturers. Dr. Bhebhe thinks about how his father eventually became a pastor and headmaster of a school, and smiles at the full-circle nature of God's open-handed leadership. Grateful for the Christian moorings his parents gave him from his birth, Dr. Bhebhe feels fortunate, blessed, and so very grateful.

There was a time when his father didn't think this day could happen. It occurred when young Stanley was expelled from the boarding school he had been attending. The abrupt uprooting brought him home to Zimbabwe and cleared the way for something new to grow. At first, he drifted without purpose. Finally, he decided to study business just so he could make a lot of money.

By 1973, Stanley Bhebhe was frustrated, aimless, and bored. Walking home one day he felt every useless pursuit and empty goal he had chased. Into that emptiness he heard his mother's words she had repeated often as a promise and a prayer, "Jesus will always accept you as His own." Stanley realized he had never tested that statement. It was about as foreign to him as life on the moon. In that moment he knew his heart was open to God in a way it never had been before. "Okay," he said as if raising his own white flag of surrender. "If this will change my life, I accept you."

That was it. No tears. No music. No preacher. No thunder. Just a decision.

Three days later, that simple decision had grown into a new life direction. He testified to it in church. It changed the trajectory of the rest of his life. He made application and was accepted into a Free Methodist Bible School. Dr. Bhebhe points to that time as "one of the most important of my life." He lived simply, studied the Bible, and memorized whole chapters. Nothing influenced his value system more than those two years. It was as if he ate and breathed everything he had missed from God.

What began in that unsophisticated Bible school took him to a Bible seminary in South Africa, to a theological college in Australia, and to doctoral work at Drew University in New Jersey, US.

Dr. Bhebhe brings great experience to the future possibilities of Africa Nazarene University. He becomes the first vice chancellor raised with Nazarene roots. His parents, originally from the Pilgrim Holiness Church, joined the Church of the Nazarene in its early days in Kenya.

He has a wealth of academic experience. He was senior lecturer at the School of Community Development and Adult Learning at the University of KwaZulu-Natal [kwah-ZOO-loo NAH tahl] in Durban [DUHR-buhn], South Africa, taught religion, ethics, and culture studies at the University of the Witwatersrand [wit-WAH-tuhrs-rand] in Johannesburg, South Africa; and served as vice rector for Academic Affairs and

> God is good to call a man to do more than he could do alone.

professor of contextual theology at Nazarene Theological College in Muldersdrift [MUHL-duhrs-drift], South Africa.

He honed his leadership style as he served in various roles in institutions and organizations, mostly in South Africa. He served at the Independent Development Trust for thirteen years[34] in South Africa in different capacities. This organization was established to give outcome-based leadership to national priorities in education, employment, poverty reduction, and health. He served as chief executive officer for World Vision-South Africa, a mobilizing entity and delivery system that helps address poverty and victimization of children and families. He also served as a member of the General Board of the Church of the Nazarene, 2006-2009.

As Dr. Bhebhe listens to the range of affirmations, vision, and blessings on the beginning of his new role as vice-chancellor, he smiles. God is good to call a man to do more than he could do alone. He scans the crowd and envisions

the possibilities God could bring. New leaders. New voices. New answers. New transformations. Yes, nothing less than transformation was acceptable.

Vice-Chancellor Stanley Bhebhe

As the new leader at ANU, he knows how to allow the past to fuel the vision for the future. "The business of today is gone, but where is the business of ANU ten years from now?" This is a question he uses to create a strategy that will take ANU into the future. "I see my role to work with people to anticipate the

[34] "VC's Citation." *Africa Nazarene University* site. www.anu.ac.ke/vcs-citation

obstacles." It is a good follow-up to the strategies that have brought ANU from 64 students to 3,600 in less than twenty-five years. He appreciates the hard-earned achievements that have helped Africa Nazarene University rank eleventh among universities in Kenya.[35] However, he would like to see the school place higher.

No one is more appreciative of the work that laid the stone path that brought him to ANU. His prior work with Nazarene higher education made him a colleague of Professor Marangu. "I can stand on her shoulders and see further," he says of her investment in ANU.

One thing that Dr. Bhebhe knows is that he came to be a transformational agent in the lives of students. "You are the reason I am here," he announced to the students gathered at the Town Campus for chapel.

Dr. Bhebhe will never separate ethics and values from education. He believes that the "marketplace requires people with some kind of value system with competence." ANU shares an ethos that goes beyond the pursuit of academic excellence. As he wears the mantle that has been placed on his shoulders, Dr. Bhebhe will continue to offer an education that builds character, competence, and community. "As they say in Africa, 'How far you go depends on the community you put around you.'" Dr. Bhebhe believes that the ANU community will help anyone go farther than they thought they could, and he wants to be part of a community that walks with them.

---

[35] "Top Universities in Kenya—2018 Kenyan University Ranking." *uniRank*. www.4icu.org/ke

There is no question in Dr. Bhebhe's mind that Africa Nazarene University is positioned for greatness. The astounding growth in enrollment, buildings, technology, and research tells so many stories of individual, national, and global involvement. He comes as the university has completed implementing a four-year strategic plan started in 2013. The school is ready for casting a new vision for the next five to ten years. In addition, they will celebrate their twenty-fifth anniversary August 2019. What better time for a new leader to begin!

While he celebrates the hard, literally backbreaking work of building this university, sometimes stone by hand-chiseled stone; he knows it is not enough. It will never be enough because a future waits. Hints of it begin to take shape, but what it will be is still a very distant image.

Who will be the leaders who have their own crisis awakening to the call of God? Who will learn the skills to communicate God's truth to the children who will be the next leaders? Will they learn more from society and protests and rebellion? Or will they learn how to build bridges and wash wounds and share hope?

"Dr. Bhebhe steps in as a spark that seeks to further flame the fire of growth of this institution," Professor John Marangu, chairman of the University Council, said at the inaugural service.[36]

Perhaps the words of Dr. Duncan Ojwang [OH-jwahng], dean of the Law School, summarized it best as he

---

[36] Marangu, John. "Message from the Chair—University Council." *Africa Nazarene University* website. www.anu.ac.ke/inauguration-message-from-chair

categorized the faculty's perception of their new leader at the inauguration:

> If you asked the School of Religion and Christian Ministry, they will tell you they...[see] Dr. Bhebhe... [as] the yeast that leavens the whole loaf of bread. If you asked the Business School, they will assure you that he is an international leader wired to lead us with grit. If you asked the School of Science and Technology, they will confirm that he is a leader who is up to date...and innovative. If you asked the School of Humanities and Social Sciences, they will indicate that he is a great communicator, a leader with *ubuntu* [oo-BOON-too][37] and he warms our hearts with powerful Africa stories! And if you asked us at the Law School, we will tell you he is a credible witness with a persuasive testimony.[38]

Dr. Bhebe leaves the Helstrom Student Centre with a new robe bearing the colors and emblem of Africa Nazarene University. He wears the graduation pillbox hat of his African heritage. It is black velvet like the darkness that wants to overtake Africa. It bears a gold brocade band like the belt of Truth he must always wear. A gold tassel dangles as the bell he must ring as a warning or reminder to make sure that ANU never loses its vision that God continues

---

[37] A Swahili word identifying a South African philosophy that focuses on group allegiance and relationship with each other. *Glosbe.* www.glosbe.com/en/sw/ubuntu

[38] Ojwang, Duncan. "Message from the Faculty Representative." *Africa Nazarene University* website. www.anu.ac.ke/message-from-the-faculty-representative

to enlarge. He carries the ceremonial golden scepter announcing that he is the new vice-chancellor for Africa Nazarene University.

Dr. Stanley Makhosi Bhebhe is Christian, Nazarene, African, husband, father, seeker of truth, purveyor of hope, and keeper of the faith.

The future of Africa Nazarene University has already begun.

Annual graduation picture at the clock tower.

Act On It

- The best way to further any part of the missional transformation at the center of the Church of the Nazarene's presence in any place in the world is through your regular contributions to the World Evangelization Fun (WEF).

- Have you sensed a tug to participate in a Work & Witness trip to Africa Nazarene University? Check out projects for Work & Witness trips on the Narative website https://serve.nazarene.org/serve/search.xhtml or contact your NMI president.

- Do you have IT skills that you could share? Visit www.globalnaz.org and fill out the form by clicking through Partner. You can also sign up for a newsletter to find out information about current needs and projects. getinvolved@globalnaz.org

- Do you have other skills in one of the highlighted areas in the book, but don't know how they might be used at ANU? Visit globalfaculty.nazarene.org and fill out the online form to submit your information.

- If you want to stay informed about what is happening at ANU, sign up to

- Receive *Friends of ANU Newsletter* by ANU at VC@anu.ac.ke

- Invite an ANU missionary to speak. For information about deputation schedules, contact scheduling@nazarene.org.